Hillside
Castle

Hillside Castle

Sandy Anderson

Illustrations by
Diane C. Moody

LEONINE PUBLISHERS
PHOENIX, ARIZONA

Published by

Leonine Publishers LLC
Phoenix, Arizona
USA

ISBN-13: 978-1-942190-52-3

Library of Congress Control Number: 2019939326

10 9 8 7 6 5 4 3 2 1

Visit us online at www.leoninepublishers.com
For more information: info@leoninepublishers.com

Dedication

✿ ✿ ✿ ✿ ✿

For my granddaughters,
Joan Catherine and Mary Anne,
Arizona girls through and through,
Tough as quartz,
Colorful as copper,
Fine as gold.

Hillside
Castle

* * * * *

Every story must have a beginning and an end. How does this one begin? In a convent school.

How will my story end? I'm not sure. It was simply a time in my life, an "interlude." That's a word that "Sol," my father, your dad's grand-father, your great-grandfather, liked to use. Sol was his nickname. It was short for his last name, Solper, a Belgian name. Sol was what his grandchildren called him. Not "Grandpa." In fact, when he and your dad and Father Tony attended the horse races together in later years, he insisted they call him "Uncle Sol!" It made him feel more sporty and more one-of-the-boys. What an interesting man he was. No wonder "interlude" was one of his favorite words! Sol's whole life was a series of interludes. Interlude for him stood for the time he was spending before he spent the next time that was waiting for him somewhere else. Each interlude was an adventure. Not all the interludes were profitable. Some were risky. And always they involved his entire family. That's the way it was in those days.

You girls may like to learn something about this interlude in Sol's life. And in my life. Your own Grammy's life. The Hillside Mine interlude.

St. Joseph's Convent and Academy was a commanding presence on the top of Murphy Hill in Prescott, Arizona. Massive and majestic as a citadel, it loomed over the town. Enclosed within this imposing palace was the throne room of the King of kings, the Eucharistic Jesus in His tabernacle in the chapel.

But St. Joseph's was also a school. Some of the children who attended classes there were boarders. Others had to walk from their Prescott homes and climb, from the east or the west, a long series of concrete steps up to the top of that hill.

Smells are important, aren't they, Mary Anne? As time goes by, sometimes the most important of our memories can be a certain smell. From St. Joseph's Academy, I remember the scent of the classroom on Monday mornings. On every other day of the few months of my fourth-grade St. Joseph adventure, I had loved the schoolroom's mingled, mysterious odors. The polished floor beneath our desks smelled shining clean, while the books, new and untattered, had their own crispy feel and smell. The big and little nuns were the kindest people in the world, and all of them smelled like soap. But on those Monday mornings...surprise! The room was always cleaner than ever, and sometimes there was a vase of roses in a window. Freshness and beauty. Even the rosary that I won in a spelling contest offered a distinctive smell. It came in its own tiny plastic box. When I opened it, there was the rosary, smelling new and plastic and *blue!* Yes, I insist that blue has a smell of its own.

But best of all, when it was the turn of our fourth-grade class to enter the chapel, we had the sweet, holy fragrance of vigil candles burning beside the altar.

From that wonderful school on its own high hilltop, from the heavenly smells and tall bright windows, from the rows of clean children at their tidy desks, from keeping company with delicious nuns who swished in their habits and whose own magnificent rosary beads rattled when they leaned over my desk, from all that fascination and serenity and order, I was cast out.

Into a canyon.

Now, imagine. Imagine little Dickie, your great-grandmother, my mother. "Grandma Dickie" was her name to your father, who knew her very well. She did not like to be called just "Grandma," and of course your father never called her that. She had always been simply "Dickie," short for her rather complicated name of Dickseay. And, of course, she wasn't a grandmother at the time of this interlude. She was a young wife and mother. Imagine a slender, delicate woman perched on a wide stiff seat inside the cab of a huge army truck, with rain pounding down and darkness coming on and the thick metal blades of the windshield wipers scraping and shrieking. A forest of levers and pedals sprouting from wide holes in the floor of cold metal was all that separated her from the roaring of the truck's engine.

Joan Catherine (Cathy), I know you don't like change. Imagine giving up a nice little house on a tidy, sloping street called Coronado, taking one of your children from her school, piling her and another small child and everything you own into a giant green truck and lumbering off into the rain.

What must Dickie have been thinking? Moving again! To a place she'd never seen. How many times? Was she "madder than a wet hen"? That was one of *her* favorite expressions. At the very least, her feathers must have been ruffled. She was like a hen in a crate, separated from her chicks. And the chicks were scattered. Out of sight behind her, under a flapping tarpaulin (tarp) lashed down against the rain, in a cave made between layers of boxes and furniture, two of her chicks huddled in the bed of the truck. One other chick, her oldest, had been left behind. This was Aunt Suzanne, only of course she wasn't an aunt in those days. She had stayed behind with our own grandmother to finish the school year. She, at least, was warm and safe.

Madder than a wet hen she might have been. But Dickie didn't squawk. She was too well-bred. Too proud. Too stubborn. And too used to vicissitude. If her feathers were ruffled, it was mostly because of the chicks.

We were the truck chicks, your dad's Uncle Bruce and I. I was nine years old and my little brother was five. For us chicks, the whole thing was a great adventure.

That truck! It smelled in there, in the half dark. It smelled of a few familiar things from our old home. It smelled of oily, waxy tarp over our heads. It smelled of gasoline. Of rain.

That truck could carry a big load. It was an army truck, built for use in World War II. U.S. Army gray-green. A troop carrier. There were long wooden benches for the soldiers on either side, but these could be folded up so it could be used for wartime construction projects. Now, with the war over, these trucks found their way into the hands of the miners. Miners loved them because they were dump trucks! Later, it was to become a wondrous sight for us when the whole back end of our truck would rise skyward on hydraulic pistons. The tailgate would swing outward and tons of rock would come rumbling down. Oh, that was a truck! It was my father's pride and joy. For us, on this moving day, it was like a great cavernous ship, carrying us to a faraway destination. We hunkered down in the passenger hold under the tarp, but it didn't take us long to discover that we could pry up flaps of canvas to peer out at the countryside. It was glorious.

In the cab of the truck, together but separate, rode my mother and father. What did they talk about? That will never be known. Just as thousands of conversations between man and wife will never be known by others. Or even remembered by themselves. These two had shared dreams and hopes. And failures. He was not a man to know how to give comfort. She was not a woman to demand it. This move was something they had to do. These were not easy times. No marriage has completely easy times. Until man and wife discover each other again in Heaven. "We talked about this," they will say. "We did this together. We suffered this other together. We laughed our way beyond many struggles. Once in a while, things turned out better than we had expected. We prayed, sometimes together, along the way. And here we are. See how it turned out. I do love you. I loved you all that time. I thank you."

Fifty or sixty miles to go now, at a clumsy, gear-shifting pace. My mother was free to perch forward for a while to help peer through the windshield, or she could try to sit back stiffly.

Not much room for her feet among the levers and pedals and whatever she must have thrown into the cab of the truck at the last minute. It was not comfortable. Dark, oil-spotted metal everywhere. No padded dashboard, no radio, no cushiony seats. No seat belts in those days. Her husband had the heavy steering wheel for support and the many levers to keep him busy, but all she could do was to shift position once in a while on purpose or *be* shifted as the truck jounced her against the metal.

Moving again. This time, to the Hillside Mine. Through Skull Valley, turn right at Kirkland, cross Kirkland Creek at Yava. Night coming on. And then there were the scattered lights of Bagdad, at the very end of a remote road in Yavapai County. But even that was not the end. One more turn and again bumping off into the darkness, to the very edge of civilization. It was still raining. We came to the brink of Boulder Canyon. Below us was the Hillside Mine. My father stopped there and they brought us into the cab of the truck. All vehicles stopped there before the final descent. You had to watch and make sure no one else was driving up from the bottom. Trucks could not pass each other on that road. It was winding and steep and dropped off sharply on one side. The ore-hauling trucks would always pause at the top to honk, to signal that they were on the way down, so that no one else would begin the haul up. On this night it was as if we were alone in the world, swaying in a lost vessel on a black sea, twisting downward into a small patch of headlight on a muddy road. I don't remember being too frightened at that time, because I had not yet seen that road in the daylight. My mother, however, must have had a pretty good idea. She had seen plenty of those narrow roads at canyon edges.

Down into the blackness we went, my father busy with the clutch and the brakes, the low gears grinding us into slowness, the windshield wipers busy, busy. We passed the shadowy nighttime bulk of the mill, and around another bend or two: lights! The road leveled out and we stopped by a little house. A young couple stepped out and my father climbed down and spoke to them. My mother stayed in the cab with us.

"Wouldn't the kiddies like a cup of hot chocolate?" a pleasant voice asked.

"No, thank you," my mother replied politely, but crisply. Dickie was always crisp when she was polite, and she was always polite. She had no idea who these people were. And I guess it was better to be polite than impolite. But how I wanted to clutch that cup of cocoa! By that time we were tired and hungry and cold, and maybe just a little damp from the leaks that had developed in the tarp.

But gears were shifted again, and that giant tortoise of a truck crawled up the sloping path to our new home.

We were able to drive right up beside the little building. There was no yard. No fence. The bright headlights of the truck picked out the odd shape of a hut sitting at the road's end on a level space carved out of the hillside. We could see the hill rising beside us, and sense that there might be still more hill dropping below. It was good to be stopped! My father left the lights on and the engine running, as he disappeared around the corner of the house to open the door for us. We were able to carry a few things inside. Just enough to get us through the night.

It was as if we had walked into a closet. Three of us stood huddled in a small room that seemed to be everything: a living room and a kitchen, with some naked boards tacked to the wall to serve as a pantry. Someone, probably my father, had made a few preparations for us. A stick or two of furniture and a cook stove. That was it. My daddy flashed a lantern around in the darkness and revealed another doorway, into a yet smaller room. Two rooms for a family of four. I don't remember what my mother said. Not much.

But Daddy turned the lantern onto the wall of the smaller room and there, inching up into the darkness, was a primitive stairway made of raw lumber, with a fresh pine smell. As the lantern picked the way up the sweet-smelling staircase, casting our shadows behind it, I followed him up into the gloom. The stairs creaked. Something moved in the lantern light. A large orange scorpion waved its tail in threat. "No," it said. "No more going up for you. These are my stairs. This is my house." Daddy smashed it with his shoe. I had to creep past the smash, skipping that step altogether. I was afraid to touch the walls that I could not see, afraid to lag too far behind my father. Later we disposed of the scorpion's remains, but for all the time we lived there I shuddered at the scorpion stain and avoided stepping on that stair.

But here Daddy and I were, up the stairs and in another tiny, empty room. The lantern's glare bounced off dark glass. A window!

Somehow, with blankets and bedrolls, Bruce and I spent the night on the floor in that room above our parents. I mostly stayed alert, listening for the pitter patter of little feet. Mice and scorpion feet. Mice there were, too! Mice eat scorpions. But I didn't know that at the time. To me all those creatures had combined forces to make a miniature army marching against us. Those were the nights,

girls, when Grammy learned to sleep lightly, like an Apache, or not at all.

But dawn will come. It always does. Windows demand looking through. Our own little window.

Oh, and glory! We were in a treehouse. Only not in a tree. Perched, indeed, we were, but perched on a bulldozed flat on the steep slope of a hillside, with the rest of the hill dropping away again as we had suspected in the night, falling a few hundred feet to where Boulder Creek wandered among its boulders. At the bottom of this plunge, close to the creek, ran a narrow dirt road. Beyond that the water gleamed.

That creek was a magnet for us.

Back down that creepy, creaky stairway we went, steering clear of the fragmented scorpion. Out of the indoor dimness into the sunlight. There was not a lot of level space between our front door and the beginning of the drop-off. We hurried over to peer down.

What was this! A bend of iron pipe signaled another set of stairs. Creeping between the rocks and prickly pear cactus and catclaw bushes, almost from our very front door it seemed, dropped a series of slender planks, descending all the way to the little road at the bottom. This stairway was even more primitive than the one up to our bird's nest bedroom. Only a rusty pipe handrail, wobbling on rusty pipe uprights could lend you any support at all as, one after the other, the twenty-seven rickety steps drew you down, down to the safe flatness of the road. And then, the creek! The miner who put all those boards and pipes together must have spent many hours making this wonderful stairway to his own private swimming hole.

Now I have to pause right here, girls, and make a confession. I really don't recall how many of those steps there were, but you can be sure that before we had made many excursions up and down them, we had counted those ancient boards more than once! Too bad that after sixty-something years I no longer remember the number. But there were a lot of them! So let's say twenty-seven. Coming back up them from the bottom when you were hot and tired, it sometimes seemed like thirty-seven! We were to know that stairway very well.

But on this first day, before we tried the stairs, to turn around and take a good daylight look back at our new home was another experience! It was a cabin, a real miner's cabin. And it was more than a treehouse cabin. It was a shoe! Remember the nursery rhyme about the old woman who lived in a shoe? She had so many children, she didn't know what to do. Remember the wonderful illustrations that went along with the poem? The shoe was usually pictured as a tall lace-up boot. That was what our cabin looked like: the two lower rooms were the foot part. The ankle part, our own bedroom loft, rose tall at one end. Only the laces were missing. If the cabin had been a real boot it would have been an old worn-out one, kind of sagging. Atop the toe, a metal tank supplied our water. We later discovered a tin cubby hole under that tank where we were expected to take our showers. If you pulled a cord on a hot day, you could have a warm shower. If it was winter time or a shady day, your shower was likely to be very short and screechy. The rest of the bathroom was a few hundred feet away. An outhouse. It was a comfortable enough place for wasps and spiders, but we spent as little time out there as possible.

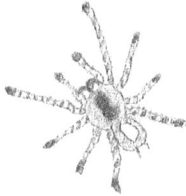

I loved that cabin from the very first day. And I loved that rickety stairway.

If I were to have a picture for my story, it would not be like anything I used to admire in my story books. There was not a magnificent marble or crystal stairway climbing to a shining palace on a peak. It was not even on a hilltop like St. Joseph's Academy. Our castle was perched on the side of a hill on a level space gouged out by a bulldozer. The hill continued to rise steeply behind us, covered with its boulders. From the creek-side below, our stairway was only a grey, gaping, wobbly ladder to a treehouse, old boot, miner's cabin. But to us it was truly a magical ladder to a magical castle. A castle on a hillside.

Sights and smells and now, sounds! What a serenade! We had not been there many days before we awoke to a "HAW!" and then a "HEE!" Then came a chorus of haws and hees, as if they were responding to each other. Sometimes they came on top of one another. The haws and hees bounced off the canyon walls and echoed among the cactus and boulders.

"Hee-haw," is how people like to describe it, but I have heard many a burro song, and it seems to me they always start with a "Haw." "Haw-hee, haw-hee, haw-hee." This quickly begins to sound like "hee-haw" and whichever comes first, a burro voice is recognizable the world over. Try it! Try saying "haw-hee-haw-hee-haw-hee-haw-hee," the way burros really say it, And you will end up thinking you are saying "hee-haw." Such a performance we began to have almost daily in that canyon, from a very small musical ensemble. But they were enthusiastic.

They came in all ages and sizes, in various shades of grey and tan, but every one of these burros had carried a cross on its shaggy body down through the centuries. Their crosses: a thin black stripe along the backbone, and a crossbeam across the withers from one shoulder to the other. The crosses are said to be a stamp upon them from the time that the motherly Mary traveled on a donkey to Bethlehem with her Joseph. There she gave birth to the baby Jesus. When the family of three had to flee into Egypt, there was the donkey again, carrying mother and baby behind Joseph to safety. When it was time for Jesus to give Himself away for us, He chose a donkey to carry Him into Jerusalem. The sign of His cross remained on the lowly burro, a royal emblem to wear proudly across his shoulders forever. Many Spanish-speaking people believe this, and I believe it, too.

How long had the burros been singing in Boulder Creek Canyon? Probably for many generations. The Arizona miners found the burros very useful. They had probably brought some of them along as pack animals, but no doubt they also found many already living in the desert. Some burro ancestors had perhaps come along with the Spanish missionaries. In the earliest days of the Hillside Mine, the sturdy, sure-footed little creatures had carried heavy loads of ore over the mountains to the railroad at Seligman.

From the first day I heard and then finally saw them, I had to have one. If you can't have a horse, then a burro is the next best thing. These burros were decidedly wild burros. Some of the old timers around the mine fed them from time to time, and they were curious and not too fearful. But they were wary! I left carrots and dry bread and handfuls of plucked grass where they could find them. I circled them at a distance. I crept up on them from behind boulders. Always, I carried my short piece of rope. I learned right away that the rope should not be seen. I would stuff it in my back pocket or keep my rope hand behind my back. I spoke to them calmly and kindly. I pleaded with them. I left my bait. I sat near them for hours, pretending to be looking only at the sky. Patience didn't work. Leaping out at them and making a dash for one of those shaggy heads certainly didn't work! My rope was never snug around a burro's neck. It's a good thing. I might have been pulled along on my stomach through the dust and cactus for quite a way. I was kind of stubborn, too. Stubborn as a burro!

As it turned out, my burros were never my burros. They were not anyone's burros. Their great-great-grandchildren are probably still roaming over Bozarth Mesa and from Boulder Creek to Burro Creek and all the way to the Big Sandy River to this day. Serenading the mesquite and the rocky hillsides and that huge, huge sky. Still free.

The Hillside Mine really was on a hillside. Mine and mill. The miners came up from the earth, from deep under the layers of rock, in a cage pulled up by cables. From darkness they emerged back into the Arizona sunlight. Their knuckles were skinned; their head lamps still glowed dimly. When they smiled, their teeth gleamed whitely out of dust-blackened faces.

The ore buckets had come up ahead of them the whole day, hoisted by the same cables.

The heavy buckets, filled with chunks of rock that the miners had blasted and picked from the walls, had been dumped into the crusher. In different stages, the ore had been battered, pounded, and crumbled until the conveyer belt could carry it into the mill. The conveyor belt, made of strong rubberized canvas, rippled along over carefully spaced rollers into the dark cavern of the mill. It was wonderful to see.

I wish now that I had paid more attention. But I do remember that the mill was a huge building that was not a building. It had a roof and a few walls with gaps wide enough to let in a lot of sky and mountain. The inside of the mill was as dusty and black as the miners' faces. It was a magical place, full of intense, scurrying men moving between giant vats of liquid. The smells were like nothing I had ever known. Damp rock. Chemicals. Pungent smells, mysterious smells. On the top of one cauldron, turquoise-colored bubbles formed, tumbled and burst, stirred by a mechanical paddle. Magical and significant was this liquid. The workers moving purposely between the machines and the cauldrons reminded me of giant, earnest elves laboring in the depths of the earth. It was fascinating. We were only occasionally permitted to go inside the mill, but I loved to linger there, standing on tiptoe beside the huge tanks, smelling the sulfurous mixture, watching the beautiful bubbles seethe and pop and form again.

Sometimes we could watch almost the whole process as the chunks of ore were turned into a powdery concentrate, which the dump trucks would haul away. Back up the scary, winding, steep road they would crawl, out of the canyon to the railroad settlement near Date Creek, to unload the concentrate onto the trains. Off into the world it would go, to become…what did it become? I don't know. The mine at Hillside had begun with the extraction of gold and silver. But other nearby mines had hauled their ore to be processed at the mill. So many, very many, *most* of the things we find so conve‑ nient in our daily lives — our cars, our refrigerators, our telephones, or at least a lot of their components — have come from boulders hacked out of the earth by elvish men with muscular shoulders, dusty faces, and white smiles.

As for those miners, the men who labored away in the tunnels under the mountain, we were not permitted to hobnob with them. My mother felt they were a rough lot, rougher than the men who guarded and checked and stirred the cauldrons. Rougher than men like my daddy, who wrote the reports and the paychecks. The mill men, especially those in charge, were a tad more civilized, a few of them perhaps better educated, than the regular miners.

The miners were mostly young single men. On their days off, they would head to Prescott, and there they would spend all their hard-earned money. Some of them never came back. Underground mining was hard and dangerous work. Looking for a paycheck, they had drifted in, worked for a single pay period, then drifted away again. "Ten-day miners," they were called by the men who stuck it out.

One of the young miners, though, had become my father's friend. There was something different about Roger Knight. He was as energetic and sometimes as rowdy as the other young men. But behind all that my parents could sense his kindness. Roger was a man who valued knowledge and contemplation. What kind of family background had he come from? How did he find his way to the Hillside Mine? He was interested in our lives, too.

"What can I bring you from town?" he once asked my brother and me.

"A horse," I said immediately. No need to think about that one!

I expected a small plastic one to add to my sizeable corral full. But Roger came back with something for Bruce, and not for me. He hadn't found a horse, he said. He asked my father if he could give me one of his own treasures, instead.

So when my daddy, "Uncle Sol," came down the hill from work one night, he brought me a gift from Roger. A pair of beautiful spurs. Mexican spurs. Crafted in a prison in Chihuahua, he said. (You will know how to pronounce Chihuahua, Cathy.) They were made from heavy blued steel and had a design of silver overlay. The straps were hand-tooled leather, and those spurs had two of the longest, jingliest rowels you could ever hope to hear.

I have never worn them for riding, because they are too heavy and elaborate. They are rusty now, but how I still love those spurs. As I write this, I say a prayer for Roger Knight. Where is he today? I am seventy-seven years old. Roger must have been at least fifteen years older than I. Could he still be alive? Roger is somewhere right now. No one ever simply ceases to exist. God knows where he is! And if Roger has died, no doubt he will still appreciate my prayers. And yours.

Roger was our friend for a good long while. Then one day he was gone. A sheriff's deputy came, after a time, to ask my father questions about him. Good, kind, sensitive, and intelligent as he had seemed to us, it turned out that he had lived an uneasy life. He had carried those spurs right out of his own prison. He himself had spent long days in a prison cell in Mexico.

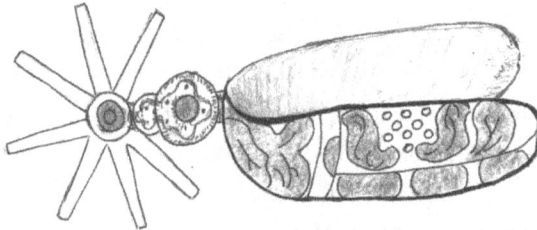

Of course, my formal education had been interrupted. I no longer had St. Joseph's Academy, but I still had my fourth grade to finish, and Bruce, small though he was, could not be left behind either. My mother became my teacher, more than she had ever been before. What fun! She had not been educated beyond high school, but she was interested in...everything. I learned the multiplication tables forwards and back-wards from the cards she held up. I had never seen the city of Montgomery, and I probably never will, but it was important to learn it was the capital of Alabama. I became familiar with the geography and cultures of other lands.

Best of all, she saw to it that we would recog-nize the beauty in whatever surrounded us. She saw everything; she really looked at everything. We learned to do the same. Bravely, in a wild over-extension of budget, she somehow secured for us our very own set of encyclopedias. Brand new they were, with thick covers in lovely green, blue, red, and brown. They made cracking noises when we opened them. The pages were very slick, and they smelled! They smelled like encyclopedias. "Books of Knowledge," they were called. The chapters were numbered in Roman numerals — something else we had to learn. Each book was surprisingly heavy, as if it contained everything in the world that you would ever need or want to know.

And guess what! I still have those books after all these years! One of them, my favorite, is missing. But here they are at Toad Hall, ten of them, still full of intriguing information, a lot of it by now surpassed or outdated, but new enough for me. They still smell, too. Now it's an older smell, musty and dusty. Yes, Grammy's books are dusty, as you have noticed! But it might be fun for you to have a peek into them one of these days.

We had lots of other books, too. On rainy days I loved to be up the stairs in that wooden-flavored room, reading my *Black Stallion* books or something by Will James. *Smokey the Cowhorse* was one of my favorites. If you looked inside the *Smokey* book, which I still have also, you might see between the pages some paper horses cut from the Western Horseman magazine in 1949. All Quarter Horses! Long before the Arabian days. Grammy has always loved horses, even paper ones! On the days when the rain came rattling on the tin roof of that wooden castle, it was glorious to be high and safe up in my sanctuary, alone with my paper horses and my dreams.

* * * * *

Try this: imagine that strange, strong, muddy smell of Boulder Creek in flood. You know how lovely is the scent of rain, right before that first drop reaches where you stand waiting. It's the freshest, sweetest, most welcome thing! It was the smell we hoped for in the dusty summer days below Bozarth Mesa. But when the rain had come and we had enjoyed it, and had relished our reading time in our cabin loft, sometimes it kept coming. And coming. Long, long rainy days.

Then suddenly the rain would stop and the clouds would lift and we would hear that other sound: the roaring approach of a mass of water down the creek. The water, trapped and channeled, would sweep away everything in its path. Boulder Creek in flood! It could wake you up at night, smashing through the canyon between the rocky mesas. In the mornings, my brother and I would go down and watch it from a respectful distance. What was happening to our tadpoles? This water now was a totally different creature. It was not our creek at all. Our creek smelled like fresh water and sunshine and mossy plants. Slightly fishy and froggy, but we could drink from it. Clear pools showed you their deepness, and in the shallow stretches the water welcomed our bare feet and lapped around our ankles. Minnows tickled our toes. But this Boulder Creek on a rampage was cocoa colored. Cocoa with a vanilla-cream foam. And the smell. It was not a chocolate smell! All the earth seemed to be suspended in its muddy waters. The waves and curls splashed high at the big rocks, rolling the smaller rocks and carrying pieces of cactus, big logs, and even green branches that had been snapped off upstream.

Sometimes we would see animals crawling up out of the water, sodden and exhausted. Once or twice we saw rattlesnakes winding away to safety.

When it was over, in a day or two or three, we would find an entirely new creek landscape. New swimming holes gouged out of the creek bed. New dams made of brush piles. Vanished beaches and water plants. New beaches. New treasures.

* * * * *

27

When my sister Suzanne was able to join us, it was easier for me to forget about the burros. Neither she nor Bruce was interested in getting dragged or trampled by one of those wild and wily creatures. And Suzanne was much more interested in the water! She has always been a water person. It was summer now, and Boulder Creek called to us. Bruce and I had mostly dabbled around in the shallow areas and looked for things on the banks, but when Suzanne came to the Hillside Mine, my mother allowed us all a bit more freedom around the water.

So down the hillside the four of us would go, almost every day, three of us taking the twenty-seven wobbly steps sometimes one step at a time, careful not to slide our bare feet across the splintery boards. Or sometimes stepping on every other board or stretching for three steps at once. Always counting, even if only in our minds. You could hold onto the rusty handrail once in a while, as you went down, but you did not want to run your hand along it or rely on it for stability. It was wobbly too, after years of keeping the stairs company. Yards and yards of it might accompany you if you tumbled down the hillside.

I say "the four of us" came down to the creek. Suzanne had brought "Judith of Yavapai" when she came to be back with the family. Judy was the purebred golden-red Cocker Spaniel who had been a birthday gift to Suzanne when she was a small girl. Judy was old now, and completely blind. But she was still happy and brave. It was impossible to make that determined little dog stay behind. Judy could not navigate the stairs, but threaded her way carefully down through the rocks and cactus behind us. It took her quite a while to rejoin us at the bottom. We always waited for her. And then, the reunion!

Everyone knows that the beloved must have a nickname. Even our dogs. If a dog has a long name, it gets shortened. That's why Michaela is Mickie. And hound Talitha is Tally. Judith of Yavapai became Judy. If a dog has a short name, sometimes it gets lengthened. Judy had to have another name at times. It was "Hoodle-Doodle!" She wiggled all over when she was happy. And her stump of a spaniel tail hoodle-doodle-doodled even faster than her chubby little body. When we all gathered at the foot of the stairs, she turned into Hoodle-Doodle! Wagging was what she was born to do. What a brave, cheerful, grand little dog. We would all troop over to the creek together, and she would plunge fearlessly into the water. She would go anywhere as long as she had our voices to follow.

Unlike Bruce and me, Suzanne was a good swimmer. She had a natural boldness around the water. Judy dog-paddled smoothly, but Bruce and I were not quite as buoyant. We swallowed a lot of water, when we tried to cross the deeper pools. Mostly we stayed in the shallow areas or bravely ducked our heads under near the shore, to look for things.

Once Suzanne was towing Bruce behind her at the end of a long cottonwood branch. The branch rolled lazily over in the water, and both Suzanne and Bruce went under. Suzanne popped up immediately, but Bruce remained out of sight. I stood in the shallows, waiting for him to reappear. But he didn't!

He remembers it this way: that he sank to the bottom and then tried to crawl up the side. He thinks I pulled him out by the hair. I remember seeing him finally come to the surface, thrashing and struggling. I couldn't swim to help him, so I thrust the branch back out to him and he grasped it, and I pulled him to shore. Suzanne might remember it a different way. She was searching for the little boy who had vanished at her end of the pool. Whatever really happened, I think that was a day that we made our way, dripping and shivering, back up the stairs rather earlier than usual. And we may not have mentioned the adventure to our mother.

* * * * *

We were a strange, but maybe typical Arizona Catholic family in those days, moving from place to out-of-the-way place. We were Catholic in history and affection, but sometimes faltering in practice. If we were staying with my grandmother in Skull Valley, we would wear hats and gloves and drive to Mass in Prescott over a twenty-mile dirt road. If we lived much farther from town or church and had unreliable transportation, we might not attend Mass for weeks. But when we lived in Prescott for that short time, of course we had Sacred Heart Church and the wonderful St. Joseph's Academy.

"Uncle" Grandpa Sol's ancestors had been in Green Bay, Wisconsin, when the Virgin Mary made one of her earthly appearances. That apparition has been officially approved by the Church. Our Lady of Good Help (as she has come to be known) revealed herself to Adele Brise in the 1800s. How I would like to go and visit her shrine. I'm thinking now that I will

33

never get there, but maybe one day you girls will be able to have that adventure.

In later years, the two Solper brothers, the first Solpers coming farther west, distanced themselves from the beautiful brick and stone churches and early day shrines of mid-America. They came to Arizona and ended up working long hours, including Sundays, at mines and ranches. Surely, they must not often have found themselves decked out in fine clothes, sitting in pews before altars at Sunday Mass.

Dickseay Jeanne, my mama, had come west, too, but she had not come so far. Born in New Mexico, she had grown up with her mother and siblings, following her engineer father from project to project, living within adobe walls with sod roofs, or in proper company housing, enjoying summer lean-tos and ramadas, watching dams rise and irrigation ditches burrow. Finally, her family landed in the wilderness of central Arizona. The father traveled often, and the rest of them would find themselves at times stranded, without a car or even any neighbors. There was no one to help Dickie's mother when her youngest brother was born in a cabin in the Bradshaw Mountains. Her oldest sister did what she could.

But whatever they endured, your great-great-grandmother, Dickie's mother, always insisted they maintain her own civilized southern Louisiana customs and manners. *They were not primitive people!*

Guardian angels are resourceful! In Arizona, in the wildest and most remote places, the two Catholic Solper brothers found Catholic wives. One young woman came from West Virginia and married the elder brother. The other bride was Dickseay, who sometimes rode with the local cowboys, and who hiked over miles of rugged roads just to go to Wagoner for the mail! She was agile and brave, but never ever once did she forget that she was a lady. She became your great-grandmother. The discovery of each other was, no doubt, for the brothers and for many others, the source of sacrament and salvation.

The children that came were baptized, and the children of those children were baptized. Little Dickie struggled to keep us close to the Holy Faith. And, from her own uncertain store of Catholic knowledge, she taught us the elements of our religion and stories of the lives of saints and heroes of the Church. She never gave up trying to instill in us the values we should carry through life.

Bruce remembers that he said his first prayers there in that treehouse cabin, a five-year-old, begging not to be carried away by flood waters that seemed to be rising to the very door. I remember standing in our loft of a bedroom with rain sheeting across the window pane and tears pouring down my cheeks, thinking of the love with which Jesus sacrificed Himself for me. That was something I had learned from the nuns. Dickie (when things went wrong, or we were hurting in some way) would often remind us to "offer it up." Offering it up became a way of life for us! A very Catholic thing to do.

Because Dickie kept the faith and imparted it to her children, your Grammy was able to pass it along to your quaint old Grandpopsie (who really wasn't quaint and old when he chose me). There is now a heroic Padre Antonio serving the Church as a missionary priest. And...there is another strong, honorable, holy man (your dad), who chose a strong and holy woman (you know who), and the two of them, out of all the children in the world, chose you, Joan Catherine, and you, Mary Anne, to become their children. (Did you notice how I have been using your new and sacramental names?) Such a set of parents! They have inspired you to (as your dad would say) "love truth, goodness, and beauty." Isn't it wonderful how all these meetings, matchings, joinings have come about? And all out of the wilds and not-so-wilds of Arizona.

None of this, of course, has been just an accident. We have the angels to bring about significant encounters. And Jesus Himself is following, always following His people to the ends of the earth. Into the barrios and dust and noise of border-town Mexico. Into the largest, brightest cities, into the crude remoteness of a mining camp, or the loneliness of a ranch's line shack. He is always pursuing, and at the same time accompanying us. Going ahead of us, too, in His Church, carrying His presence in word and sacrament.

When our family finally did leave the Hillside Mine, which was mostly a network of underground and invisible tunnels, and moved into the little town of Bagdad, perched at the edge of a huge open-pit copper mine, where layers and layers of mountainside lay exposed, there Jesus was, ahead of us, waiting in humble St. Francis of Assisi Church. Waiting for us in His Holy Eucharist.

See Him! Behold the Lamb of God! Look at what has come to Bagdad, Arizona, of all places. Bagdad, a town the size of a mustard seed. Seeking His people, even here. Feeding His sheep. The baby in the manger, the transfigured Christ, the Christ on the Cross, the resurrected Christ. How great and generous He is. And yes, how humble to remain here, as He is. In the Blessed Sacrament.

* * * * *

It was not an easy life, I suppose, for my mother. She had grown up having to be Arizona tough, and she had a strong sense of adventure and discovery, but at the same time, when I knew her, she *was* a mother. She was concerned for our manners, our health, our safety, our education, and our *souls*. After a year or so, or a year or less, she prevailed upon my father to let us move the six or seven miles into the "big city" of Bagdad. There we could attend Mass more regularly, go to a real school, and live in a real house with a real shower and a real toilet, and a real kitchen with a real *refrigerator*. You girls don't understand how handy it is to have a refrigerator!

But before we left the Hillside Mine and my wonderful old boot, treehouse, miner's cabin castle, my mother took Bruce and me on a grand pilgrimage. She planned to *walk* to Bagdad on an old burro trail over the hills between the two mining camps. It would make a two-mile short-cut out of the seven rugged road miles. Someone had directed her carefully, told her she couldn't miss the trail, that it was easy to spot. But miss it we did. We followed Boulder Creek downstream for a couple of miles. We were supposed to find the trail to our left, heading south across the mesa. We walked on and on.

At first, we were quite enthusiastic and adventuresome. We wandered along beside the beautiful creek farther than we had ever gone before. My mother was as interested in the sights, sounds, and smells as we were. But, finally she began to worry. We should have found the cut-off trail. Now it was a long way back to our Hillside Castle, and Bruce was getting very tired. We trudged on. My poor mother. On her own, it might not have been so much of a challenge. But she had also to manage two young children.

Maybe little Dickie knew enough about the geography to remember Copper Creek, or maybe we just stumbled upon it. But there it was, the little stream that came trickling down from Bagdad to empty itself into Boulder Creek. It was good to see some buildings at that confluence, and a pumping station to lift water up the hill to the mine and town. And, best of all! A little dirt road ran northeast along the creek in the direction of Bagdad. It was not much of a road, but obviously some people lived down here, because we saw a shack and some cows and corrals, although we did not see a human being.

Now, finally, we did turn left. Coming along Boulder Creek we had ambled steadily downhill. But suddenly the road beside Copper Creek took us in a different direction. And it was up. On we went. Our feet were dragging, and a rainstorm was threatening. Then it was upon us! We were soaked immediately and looking to be much wetter. Our clothes were plastered to our bodies. A desert drenching can cause your teeth to rattle! We kept walking and shivering, hardly able to see. But our mama was looking out for us.

And God takes care of His children. My mama was His little child too, don't forget. She pulled her babies into a rough, three-sided shed of weathered boards, and we huddled there with the rain hammering on the sheets of tin overhead. In front of us the water poured off the roof in waterfalls so heavy we could not see through them, and the shed was smelly and dirty. But for a time it, too, was like a castle to us.

However, it was not *our* castle! It turned out that, like Goldilocks, we were only intruders. Papa Bear, Mama Bear, Baby Bear, and their relatives came home to find us there. Only they were not bears. They were pigs! Real pigs. Snuffling, snorting and grunting, in they came. We were not sitting in their chairs or eating their porridge, but we *were* taking up their space.

They did not accuse us of trying out their beds, but they bustled about bickering among themselves and shouldering each other, glancing suspiciously at us out of squinty eyes and looking as though they would be glad to shoulder *us*. They were very wet and cold and somewhat cross. Pigs have very little hair and very little patience.

We were cornered against the back of the pen. Little Dickie had no experience with pigs. You didn't see them often in the canyons of Arizona. But these animals were large and proprietary, and Dickie's children were small. Her instincts told her that it would be better not to annoy those pigs. Somehow, she herded us against the walls of the shed and around to the front opening, back out into the rain. The pigs remained triumphantly at home.

We started up the road to Bagdad again. The rain was slowing, and soon stopped. The sun came out suddenly, as it does in Arizona: "Jolly, round, red Mr. Sun," as we like to say in our family. Of course, Thornton Burgess had said it first in his *Old Mother West Wind* stories. But we were very, very glad to see that jolly sun.

Still, there we were, on a soggy steaming road with tiny rivulets winding down, facing the long climb up Copper Creek Canyon to the tailings ponds of the Bagdad mine and on, still upward, to the settlement itself, and from there... sometime...across the mesa and back down into our own canyon to the pot of beans my mother had left slowly simmering on the stove.

We were very hungry by this time. I could almost smell those beans. Frijoles! Pinto beans! She had probably even put a bit of bacon in them. They seemed a long way away.

But somewhere, either along that Copper Creek road or on the road from Bagdad to our own mine, some Good Samaritan had stopped to gather our little rag-tag group into his truck. Bruce remembers it as someone going from Bagdad on to the Hillside Mine, but I do definitely remember walking on that final lap of the trip. We were still on foot for quite a stretch.

I remember my mother's encouragement. "Oh, look," she would say. "There's alligator rock," or, "There's that funny, twisted juniper where we saw the hawk with the snake," or something about some other familiar landmark. She had to work hard to keep us going. Bruce would stop, crumple up on his five-year-old legs and sit down on the ground.

Little Dickie must have been exhausted herself, but she kept smiling and cheering us on. "We can offer this up!" she probably said at least once. And maybe that is where and when we finally got the ride. I think I do remember being in a stranger's truck when we reached the top of the switchbacks. I think I remember a loud and cheerful honking as we started down. I seem to see my father standing at the bottom of the hill, waving at us as we crept down the mountainside. How would he know it was us? We had no cell phones! But there he was, joyful and horribly worried and telling my mother that she should never do such a thing again. As if she would want to! We had walked perhaps eight or nine miles. We were hours and hours overdue. He did not know if we were still somewhere along Boulder Creek, or if we had made it over the shortcut to Bagdad. Where, and how, could he have set out to look for us?

And then we went home together. The beans had given up on us and had glued themselves, a black-ened, solid mass, onto the bottom of the pot.

* * * * *

Girls, there is something about a *place*. You will find different places in your lives. Some of them will mean more to you than others. Some of them you will forget until the way a certain shaft of light comes through the trees, the song of a particular bird, a *smell*, even, will bring back a memory of a moment when your body *was* somewhere. It *was,* and it was *real*. It was alive in a place and you were in it, and your feet were solid upon a piece of ground and the ground was yours, because God wanted you to be there at that time. You.

Some places will capture you. A piece of your heart will belong there. Even if you move on, which you will from time to time, that place will remain in your mind and imagination, in your soul. And when you slip beyond this life and into God's eternal Kingdom, He might surprise you with the gift of being there again, or a better way to say it, of drawing that place with you into His own great reality. (Grammy does have some novel ideas.) Or maybe not so novel.

The mystic Adrienne von Speyr says this about our familiar world:

> *God's creation…at the end of time will flow into eternity — not to disappear, but to make eternal in God everything that happened during the temporal days and nights, according to God's design.*

So, the Hillside Mine is one place Grammy will keep and remember. One interlude. The castle cabin, the miners, the books, the wobbly stairway down the hill, the creek, the burros. My good parents. And when you remember Grammy, remember her remembering this. And you can be there with her, and she will be happy to share with you someday your own good "rememberies" (as your father used to say).

* * * * *

Not quite the end.

Epilogue

· · · · ·

Yes, I know. In later years Boulder Creek suffered from contamination by mine and mill refuse. The diggings themselves were considered blemishes on the landscape. After its closure, the Hillside Mine became a source of environmental embarrassment.

The old miner's cabin/boot castle itself was bulldozed away.

A shadow of sorrow, and even possibly regret, flavors our most memorable experiences. Everything is passing, everything changing. But for a magical time for me, an interlude, the mine enterprise was a setting of beauty and innocent adventure.

There was an element of innocence, too, among the men who developed Hillside and risked their fortunes and at times their very lives over it. The land was a difficult, resisting country. It required a mighty labor, persistent hope, and a great deal of self-sacrifice. The challenge was monumental. The men did not spend a lot of time providing remedies for the long-range impact of their efforts. Perhaps they did not even consider that.

Nowadays more care is taken to do the least amount of damage with our major human endeavors. But not always. Even now we deceive ourselves if we condemn those brash, creative, courageous miners.

Everything we do, everything we need, or think we need, costs the earth something. To deny our part in this would be dishonest.

This world will always be an imperfect place. Metals still have to be extracted, trees felled, dams and highways built, cattle butchered, and meadows plowed. Even the reclamation of the Boulder Creek area is imperfect. In our lifetimes it will never be quite the same as when it was created.

But there is hope. Our whole life is a pilgrimage, an interlude! God has promised us a new heaven and a new earth. And if God can restore our very bodies to their original glory, certainly He can restore the wounded earth, if He chooses.

✧ ✧ ✧ ✧ ✧

"Creation itself will be set free from its bondage to decay and attain the glorious liberty of the children of God."

Romans 8:21

About Leonine Publishers

Leonine Publishers LLC makes fine Catholic literature available to Catholics throughout the English-speaking world. Leonine Publishers offers an innovative "hybrid" approach to book publication that helps authors as well as readers. Please visit our web site at www.leoninepublishers.com to learn more about us. Browse our online bookstore to find more solid Catholic titles to uplift, challenge, and inspire.

Our patron and namesake is Pope Leo XIII, a prudent, yet uncompromising pope during the stormy years at the close of the 19th century. Please join us as we ask his intercession for our family of readers and authors.

Do you have a book inside you? Visit our web site today. Leonine Publishers accepts manuscripts from Catholic authors like you. If your book is selected for publication, you will have an active part in the production process. This book is an example of our growing selection of literature for the busy Catholic reader of the 21st century.

www.leoninepublishers.com